We Celebrate
Winter

Bobbie Kalman

Susan Hughes

Brenda Clark   Elaine Macpherson

The Holidays & Festivals Series

Crabtree Publishing Company

The Holidays and Festivals Series
Created by Bobbie Kalman

Writing team:
  Bobbie Kalman
  Susan Hughes

Illustrations:
  Color illustrations by Brenda Clark
  Black-and-white illustrations by Elaine Macpherson
  © Crabtree Publishing Company

Editor-in-Chief:
  Bobbie Kalman

Editors:
  Susan Hughes
  Maria Casas
  Jo-Anna Boutilier

Art direction and design:
  Elaine Macpherson Enterprises Limited

Acknowledgments:
  "Way Down South" (pages 46-47)
  Music by Jerry Brodey
  Used by permission.

For Peter

Cataloguing in Publication Data
Kalman, Bobbie, 1947-
  We celebrate winter

(The Holidays and festivals series)
Includes index.
ISBN 0-86505-046-5 (bound)
ISBN 0-86505-056-2 (pbk.)

1. Winter - Folklore - Juvenile literature.
2. Festivals - Juvenile literature. I. Hughes, Susan,
1960- . II. Clark, Brenda. III. Macpherson, Elaine
IV. Title. V. Series.

GT3933.K34 1986   j398'.33

350 Fifth Ave., Suite 3308
New York, N.Y. 10118

360 York Road, R.R.4
Niagara-on-the-Lake, Ontario L0S 1J0

73 Lime Walk
Headington, Oxford OX3 7AD

Contents

4

Old Man Winter

Old Man Winter is a fascinating guy.
His long, white beard sweeps across the sky,
Adding sparkles to the snowflakes that gently float
And cover the ground in a velvet coat.
Yeah, I love that winter,
Whee, I love that snow!

Old Man Winter has a hold on me.
He brings my favorite time of year, you see!
I hurry outside and put on my skis.
I shoot down that hill as fast as I please!
Yeah, I love that winter,
Whee, I love that snow!

Old Man Winter makes me clomp and romp.
With my big snowshoes, through the woods I stomp,
Or sometimes I glide on a cross-country run.
Winter is a time for exercise and fun.
Yeah, I love that winter,
Whee, I love that snow!

When Old Man Winter blows a white wonderland,
My friends and I have something special planned.
We build a snow fort or feed the birds.
We sing songs about ice or write winter words!
Yeah, we love that winter,
Whee, we love that snow!

Old Man Winter makes our cheeks all red.
After whizzing down hills on our big wooden sled,
We go back inside where it's cozy and warm
And sip hot chocolate as we watch the snowstorm.
Yeah, we love that winter,
Whee, we love that snow!

Winter is on its way

The leaves have fallen from the trees. The air is starting to get colder.
Animals are growing their winter coats. We put away our summer clothes
and get out our winter woolies. We need boots, hats, scarves, mittens, and
coats to keep us warm now!

The winter spirit

Do you live in a place that has a snowy winter? How do you feel when
winter arrives? Do you bundle up and run outside to make the first
footprints in the snow? Do you roll down a hill and stand up looking like
a snowman? Do you smell the crisp, cool air and catch snowflakes on your
tongue?

Get into the winter spirit! Slide on the ice or jump into a snowdrift. Make
a snow house and invite your friends in for a visit. Write giant messages
in the snow with footprints. Look for animal or bird tracks. Make up a
poem or a song to describe how you feel about winter.

When is winter?

The first day of winter is called the winter solstice. Winter comes to the
northern half of the world around December 21. The solstice is the
shortest day of the year. It has more hours of darkness than hours of light.
The sky is dark when you wake up in the morning and dark when you go
to bed. After the solstice, the days become longer. We have more minutes
of light each day. Many people around the world celebrate because the
solstice is the beginning of the end of darkness.

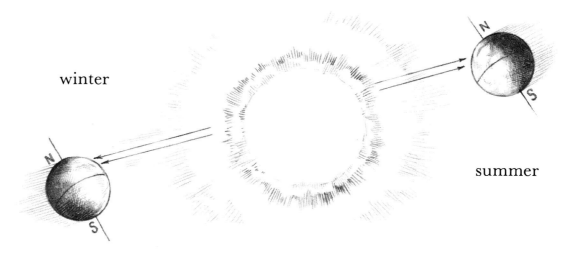

winter

summer

The winter season ends in late March. The first day of spring is March 20 or 21. It is called the spring equinox. By this time, the days have become much longer. On the equinox, day and night have the same number of hours. Then the spring days become longer than the nights.

A daylight calendar

Make a daylight calendar and discover the patterns of daylight. Begin several weeks before the winter solstice. On each day, mark down the exact time the sun rises and sets. (You can check the newspaper or listen to the radio for these times.) At the end of each day, add up the number of hours and minutes of daylight. This will be the amount of time between sunrise and sunset. Is the period of light greater or smaller than the period of darkness in a twenty-four-hour day?

Continue the calendar until the end of January or longer. What did you discover? Did the day of the solstice have a fewer number of daylight hours than any other day? After the solstice, did the number of daylight hours increase or decrease? Can you see a pattern in the figures you have collected?

Cold, hot, wet, or dry?

Did you know that when it is winter in North America, it is summer in Australia and New Zealand? When it is winter in Australia and New Zealand, it is summer in the northern part of the world. In some places such as the southern part of the United States, the Caribbean, South America, and Africa, it rains more during some parts of the year, but it never snows!

Would you rather live in a place with or without snow? Why? What would you do during a season of rain? Find out how people celebrate winter in both cold and warm places!

The Ice Queen

Slowly, she walked across the snow. Her long, silver gown glistened. Her glass crown sparkled. The snowflakes caught in her flowing hair and twinkled like precious gems. A single tear rolled down her cheek and turned to ice. Krystella, the Ice Queen, took winter with her wherever she went, and wherever she went, the birds and animals would hide. Krystella sighed sadly and wrapped her gown closely around herself.

Suddenly, she heard a quiet, mysterious voice say, "Close your eyes." When Krystella opened them again, she gasped. She saw a beautiful, green world around her! The sun was shining brightly on a rainbow of colorful flowers. She heard birds singing and bees humming. She smelled the beautiful, rich earth. She had never before seen summer and she wondered now how she had ever lived without it.

"This is a land of never-ending summer. Here, there is no winter," the quiet voice said. The Ice Queen smiled and walked in the soft, warm breezes of the meadow, picking daisies and bluebells as she went. She wanted to stay here forever. Because Krystella was invisible, she was able to listen unseen to the children who were playing in the meadow. She was surprised to hear them telling stories about a cold place where the earth was covered in a blanket of white. In this magical land, children slid across frozen lakes on blades of shiny steel. They made angel prints and figures of snow. The children dreamed of visiting this marvelous place.

Krystella was amazed. The children were wishing for winter! They were actually dreaming of snow and ice. Krystella could help these children's dreams come true, even if it meant she would have to say good-bye to summer forever. She closed her eyes. When she opened them, everything was white. The children cheered with glee! The Ice Queen's hair again twinkled with snowflakes. "How lucky I am to be able to take winter with me wherever I go," she said. Krystella smiled proudly as she spread her snowy cloak across the land.

Will spring ever return?

At the beginning of winter, we think about the fun we will have in the snow. We imagine the games we will play. We think of all the good things that come with winter. But sometimes we cannot help thinking that, however much we enjoy winter, it's good to know that spring will soon follow. At the beginning of winter, spring seems so far away. Does it ever seem to you that spring will never return?

Long, long ago, people were afraid that when winter began, spring would not return. They could not enjoy the winter season unless they were certain it would end in a few months. So, each winter they lit bonfires to remind the sun to return in the spring. They hung evergreen branches on the outside of their homes to remind the plants to grow again.

A Yule yell

Yule was one of the old winter festivals. It was celebrated in December by the Vikings who lived in northern Europe. The Vikings wanted to bring light to the cold and dark time of year. They gave a great shout or yell to the gods and asked them to bring back the sun.

The Vikings lit huge bonfires using great logs. The burning logs were a sign that the light of spring would return when winter ended. People stood drinking and feasting around the fires. They believed that the ghosts of the dead came looking for food at this time of the year. Food and drinks were put out for them. Everyone listened to the poets sing old songs and legends. Yule was a happy time of the year!

Saturnalia

More than two thousand years ago, the Romans, who lived in southern Europe, also held a special celebration each December. They, too, wanted to make sure that the winter would not last long and the sun would shine brightly again. They held a festival for Saturn, the Roman god of farming. They prayed to Saturn to make the crops grow the following year.

The festival was called Saturnalia. Saturnalia lasted for seven days. People paraded through the streets wearing masks and animal skins. Schools were closed. Friends visited one another and exchanged good-luck gifts such as clay dolls, cakes, fruit, and wax candles. The temples were decorated with evergreen branches.

A topsy-turvy time

Does being wrapped up in layers of winter clothing make you grumble? Maybe you find yourself spending a lot of time sitting inside because it is too cold to play outside. Maybe you feel that you are not ready for the long months of snow and ice which lie ahead. In the winters of long ago, the Romans must have felt this way, too. They wanted to kick up their heels and ignore the cold. They wanted to feel free of winter!

A special tradition was started. During the seven days of Saturnalia, people traded places with their servants. They exchanged clothes and duties. The masters served food to the servants. The servants could do and say whatever they liked! This topsy-turvy time was a fun way to turn the tables on the winter blahs.

Upside-down fun!

Have a Saturnalia day in your home. Ask the members of your family to exchange roles with one another for a few hours, an afternoon, or a whole day. What will happen when everything is turned topsy-turvy? What pranks might your parents play when they pretend to be your children?

Feet up, hands down

Have upside-down races. Mark off a starting place and a finishing point. On the word "Go," all the players must somersault as quickly as possible to the finishing point. Be careful not to get too dizzy!

Try another upside-down race. Each player finds a partner. The first partner holds the second partner's feet while the second partner walks on his or her hands. If they "wheelbarrow" to the finish point before the other pairs do, they will win hands down!

Upside-Down Pineapple Cake

Serve your friends and family the perfect Saturnalia treat, an Upside-Down Pineapple Cake!

Pineapple topping
60 mL (1/4 cup) butter
125 mL (1/2 cup) firmly-packed brown sugar
250 mL (8 ounces) pineapple rings
7 maraschino cherries

Preheat oven to 180°C (350°F). Melt butter and pour into a round cake pan. Sprinkle brown sugar evenly over butter. Place one pineapple ring in center of pan. Cut other rings in half and place in circle around center ring. Put one cherry in each half-ring.

Batter
310 mL (1 1/4 cups) all-purpose flour
250 mL (1 cup) sugar
8 mL (1 1/2 teaspoons) baking powder
185 mL (3/4 cups) milk
80 mL (1/3 cup) margarine
1 egg
5 mL (1 teaspoon) vanilla

Put all ingredients into a large bowl and beat well until smooth. Pour over pineapple rings. Put cake in oven and bake 35-45 minutes. When done, turn cake over onto plate. Your Upside-Down Cake is ready to serve after it is cool.

Dressing down

Have an upside-down parade with your family and friends. Wear your clothes inside out. Put your shoes on your hands and your gloves on your feet. Draw an upside-down face on a paper bag. Cut out the mouth and put on your upside-down mask. You are now looking through the mouth! Talk backwards as you parade. Put a little water in a balloon, blow it up, and tie it shut. Attach a piece of string. The balloon will dangle down from the string. Carry your upside-down balloon. What a crazy winter parade this will turn out to be!

Feast of Fools

The British celebrated a festival similar to Saturnalia. They called this festival the Feast of Fools. Just as in Rome, the masters traded places with their servants. This was a time for merrymaking. It was a time to play foolish pranks. Everyone had a good time and started the winter off with happy feelings!

The leader of mischief

The Lord of Misrule was in charge of the mischief. He wore a fancy costume of brightly colored stockings, leather boots, and a hat with feathers. He carried a staff which was topped with a fool's head wearing a cap and bells. The Lord of Misrule led a parade of giants, dragons, goblins, bears, and other fantastic animals. Mother Goose and Robin Hood were also a part of this strange procession!

When the Lord of Misrule tapped his staff, the bells jangled loudly. This meant it was time for all adults and children to show just how foolish they could be. And then the fun really began!

Christmases of long ago

Almost two thousand years ago, Christians began to celebrate the birth of Jesus Christ. Each year, the Christmas celebrations began on December 25. They lasted for twelve days. People thanked God for sending Jesus to earth.

Christmas was celebrated at the same time of year as Yule and Saturnalia. People who became Christians kept many of the old winter traditions as a part of their Christmas celebrations. They carried on some of the Yule and Saturnalia customs such as burning Yule logs, having fun, and feasting. They also decorated their homes with evergreens and holly.

A medieval Christmas

In the medieval days of knights and castles, Christmas became a huge celebration. Can you imagine a medieval Christmas? Let's celebrate one together!

Bringing in the Yule log

Bringing in and burning the Yule log is an important part of our medieval Christmas celebration. Come into the woods with us to search for the perfect tree. Join in with our carol singing as we cut down the tree and trim its branches. Now it is our Yule log! Sprigs of evergreen and holly decorate our log.

Can you see little Arthur riding on the log with holly in his hands? He squeals happily as we drag the Yule log out of the forest by ropes. A young boy carrying a lighted torch leads our procession to the banquet hall.

Lighting the Christmas spirit

Listen to the cheers as the huge log is lit with a piece of last year's log. The Yule log will burn during the twelve days of Christmas. We put aside a small piece of it so we can light next year's Yule log with it. We save this piece to make sure the spirit of Christmas will stay with us throughout the year.

Time for feasting

Sit down at the table with us and enjoy the Christmas feast. Sample the many delicious foods. And now comes the highlight of the evening! Hold your breath as the trumpeters, four carolers, and two hunters enter the banquet hall. They are preparing the way for the Boar's Head. It is carried in on a silver platter. It has an apple in its mouth. Let us sing when we see this wonderful sight!

''The Boar's Head in hand bring I,
With garlands green and rosemary;
I pray you all sing merrily!''

Christmas, a special day for me

Christmas is here! Let us sing
Of the joy and smiles this day will bring.
We remember Jesus in the stable born
So long ago on this very morn!
Wise men and shepherds before him knelt;
Wonder and love for him they felt.

Now we, with friends and family dear,
Celebrate this special day of the year.
Around the tree we first sit talking,
Then we peek inside our Christmas stocking
Hung by the chimney for Santa to fill.
What wonderful treasures out of it spill!

We open our gifts from under the tree —
Toys and books for you and me!
The Christmas turkey begins to cook.
Peek in the oven for a quick look.

Now at the table we all meet.
The Christmas meal we begin to eat:
Turkey and turnip, potatoes and peas.
Soon the Christmas crackers we seize
And pull with pops! and snaps! and bangs!
We run to the room where the mistletoe hangs
To give Christmas kisses to everyone
And end a day of Christmas fun!

Knut's Day is here!

"Get ready!" Berit cried.

Berit and her friends stood around the Christmas tree. They had taken down all the decorations and stored them away for the next year. All that remained on the tree were the candies and cookies that had been put up before Christmas.

"Get set!" Berit called.

Berit was sorry that Christmas was over, but she loved January 13. It was Knut's Day, and children all over Sweden were having parties.

"Go!" shouted Berit and her friends. They leaped at the tree. It was time to "plunder!" Down came the caramels! Down came the ginger biscuits! Down came the sugar cookies! And then all that was left were crumbs on the corners of everyone's mouth.

"And now," said Ingmar, "we must say good-bye to the tree." Down it came. The children carried it outside, singing:

"Christmas has come to an end,
And the tree must go.
But next year once again,
We shall see our dear old friend,
For he has promised us so."

21

Eight days of Hanukkah

Hanukkah is a Jewish celebration which usually comes in December. This holiday celebrates peace. Jews remember a time when they fought for their religion over two thousand years ago. They fought for three years before they won the freedom to follow their beliefs.

After their victory, the Jews wanted to give thanks to God for their freedom. They gathered around the holy menorah in their Temple. The menorah was a tall, golden candlestick with seven branches. Each branch had a cup which was filled with oil. The oil was always supposed to be burning.

The miracle of the oil

On this special day of celebration, the Jews lit the oil in the menorah. Even though there was only enough oil for one day, the menorah stayed lit for eight days. A miracle! In honor of this eight-day miracle, the Hanukkah menorah now has eight branches and eight candles (plus one for the shamash, the candle that is used to light the eight candles.) How many days do you think the celebration of Hanukkah lasts? Right! Eight days!

Many Jewish children celebrate Hanukkah by lighting the candles of their menorahs. During these special eight days, they enjoy storytelling, gift-giving, wonderful dinners, and games.

A story of peace

Hanukkah has come. Let us light
The first candle of the menorah tonight.
Eight happy days have just begun;
It's time for family, friends, and fun.
We have a big meal (I like latkes best!),
Then we kids play games while the grownups rest.
Later, by the menorah, Grandma tells a story
Of a battle, of peace, and of a time of glory.

Happy New Year

When does New Year come? The Chinese celebrate it in January or early February. Jews celebrate Rosh Hashanah or New Year in autumn. Muslims celebrate New Year on a different day each year. Many people celebrate New Year on January 1. When do you celebrate the new year?

Grandfather Frost, a Russian Santa

In Russia, New Year's Day is one of the biggest holidays of the year. Children look forward to it with great excitement. When they wake up on New Year's morning, they find presents under a decorated tree. Ded Moroz has left these presents. Ded Moroz is Grandfather Frost. He has a long, white beard and wears a velvet coat. The children celebrate his arrival by going outdoors and having fun in the winter weather. They go skating or sledding. Some of them ride through the park in a horse-drawn troika. Then they wave good-bye to the invisible visitor, Ded Moroz, who is setting off on his way north!

Winter words

Try to use all these words in your own story about winter.

holly

cross-country skiing

troika

snowshoes

snow sculpture

Boar's Head

Bonhomme

curling

Yule log

stone

broom

26

bobsled

mistletoe

mask

kamakura (snow hut)

skijoring

fifer

downhill skiing

snowflake

steel drum

Santa Claus

gondola

toboggan

menorah

27

Gifts for the animals

In the winter in many European countries, children go to the park
or into the woods and leave gifts of food for the animals. They
sometimes string up nuts or leave pieces of suet on the tree branches.
The animals enjoy these winter treats!

A celebration of nature

The birds that live in cold, snowy lands often have trouble finding food in the winter months. Would you like to help them? Make a winter snack for the birds. Have a parent or an older friend help you melt suet or bacon fat. Mix it with wild birdseed or peanut butter. Let it harden, and roll it in raisins, crumbs, and small pieces of cheese. Put it into a margarine tub or paper cup. Poke holes in the container and use string to hang it from a tree. You can also roll pine cones in the mixture and hang the cones from the trees. Then listen to the happy chirping of the birds that share their colors and songs with you all year round.

A treat for the squirrels

What about those hungry squirrels? Maybe they have not stored enough nuts for the winter! Leave out food for them, too. Nuts and seeds make great squirrel snacks. Perhaps you have seen rabbit tracks in the snow near your home. Rabbits enjoy leafy vegetables, carrots, and beans.

Thanking the trees

Do you enjoy seeing the trees covered in snow? They look as though they are dressed in warm winter robes! Trees give you blossoms in the spring and shade in the summer. Some trees give you fruit in the autumn. Have your own day of thanking the trees for these gifts.

Pretty gifts

Make chains using colorful paper. Use a long, blunt needle to string popcorn and cranberries on thread. Decorate the trees around your home with these special gifts!

A toast to nature

In Britain, January 6 was a night for thinking about nature. Farmers went out to their orchards or forests. They gathered around the largest, oldest tree which had given them years of apple, peach, plum, or pear crops. They sang songs to the tree. They did a stamping dance to remind the tree to reawaken in the spring. They drank a hot, spicy cider called wassail. The name wassail comes from the words ''Waes Haeil,'' which means ''Be happy and healthy.'' The farmers wished the tree good health! This wassailing ceremony is still performed in some parts of Britain today.

Wassail

Make some wassail and drink a toast to nature!

1 L (4 cups) sweet cider   12 whole cloves
125 mL (1/2 cup) sugar   a dash of allspice
5 cinnamon sticks

Heat ingredients in a pot until almost boiling. Turn off heat and let wassail stand for several hours. Remove cinnamon sticks. Reheat before serving.

A wild time!

It is the middle of winter and the streets are full of strange-looking creatures! In Austria, ghostly witches and phantoms sing songs and beat drums as they parade. In Basel, Switzerland, hundreds of drummers and fifers march through the city at dawn. They wear eerie masks and frightening outfits. After months of stitching and sewing, people in Rio de Janeiro, Brazil, parade in their colorful costumes to the rhythm of swinging bands.

What is going on? It's Carnival time! Carnival is celebrated before Lent in many countries. Lent is the period of forty days that leads up to the Christian holiday, Easter. The word Carnival comes from the Latin language and means "to take away meat." During Lent, many Christians stop eating meat because they believe that Jesus did not eat at all during this time. Carnival is a time of feasting and festivities before the forty days of fasting and prayer.

Mardi Gras

In New Orleans, carnival time is called Mardi Gras. Mardi Gras means Fat Tuesday. Fat Tuesday is the last day before Lent and is usually in February. On this day, people try to use up all the fat in their homes because they will not use fat during Lent. People from all over the world come to New Orleans to celebrate Mardi Gras. Balls are held almost every night from Christmas until Fat Tuesday. Parades continue day and night. Everyone dances to the toe-tapping sounds of the jazz bands.

Carnival in Venice

In Venice, Italy, people travel from place to place in special boats called gondolas. During Carnival, lords and ladies of long ago, clowns, and bizarre animals ride in gondolas and parade in the city square.
The restaurants are filled with adults and children dressed in costumes. There are big parties and balls in the palaces. The museums show special Carnival exhibits. The whole city of Venice swings with the rhythm of Carnival.

Celebrating the snow

On the first day of February in Sapporo, Japan, everyone begins to celebrate the winter with a spectacular snow festival called Yuki Matsuri.

Before the festival, trucks carry thousands of loads of snow to the main square of Sapporo. Huge blocks of ice are cut from the frozen rivers nearby and are hauled to the square. Two thousand workers are hired to make sculptures of the snow and ice. They mold and chip. They make figures of famous people, ice castles, spaceships, trains, and other fabulous objects. Some of the sculptures are enormous!

Many, many people visit Sapporo during this snow festival. For four days, they watch skiing and skating contests. They admire the sculptures and enjoy the beautiful parades. Everyone who visits Sapporo during the snow festival gets a glimpse of the best part of winter!

Yoshida's favorite day

My name is Yoshida. I live in the town of Yokote in Japan. In my town, we have a special winter celebration called Kamakura. It is my favorite day of the year. My sister and I run outside and choose a huge snowdrift by our home. We hollow it out. We cover the floor of our hut or kamakura with a thick straw mat. We make small shelves in the walls and place lighted candles on them.

My sister and I leave our shoes outside. We sit on the mat in socks and slippers and wrap ourselves in thick quilts. We heat small rice cakes over a little charcoal stove.

Our parents and neighbors come to visit us. We offer them rice cakes and little cups of sweet wine. They leave fruit or coins in return. If we are lucky, we are allowed to spend the night in our kamakura!

35

Winter way up north

The winter in northern Europe, Canada, and Alaska is long and snowy. Sometimes this season seems to last forever. In the far north and south, it is dark for most of the winter! To make the time pass more quickly, families and friends who live in these areas gather for mid-winter celebrations. They cook up feasts of reindeer, seal, and walrus meat. They beat drums and chant. Then the dancing begins!

Racing, tugging, kicking, and bouncing

The Inuit, who live in the Canadian north, have canoe races in the cold, icy water. They play many games such as High Kicks, Kneel-and-Jump, and Tug-of-War. One of their favorite games is Blanket Toss. Several men hold the sides of a large hide or blanket. They toss a jumper high into the air. As long as the jumper stands upright, the tossing continues. When the jumper does not land on his or her feet, it is someone else's turn!

36

Away we go!

In the old days, the Inuit used dog sleds to travel over the snow. Some of the people who live in the far north still use dog sleds. Teams of five, seven, or nine dogs pull the sled. One dog is the leader and the others pull in pairs. The driver of the sled is called the musher.

There are many dog-sled races held in the north during the winter carnivals. One of these is called the Yukon Quest. Teams race from Fairbanks, Alaska, to Whitehorse, Yukon. This a long way to travel in the dark winter days without sunlight!

Hitching up the reindeer

In Lapland, northern Scandinavia, some of the mountain people use reindeer to pull their sleighs. Some reindeer can also be trained to carry packs on their backs!

Imagine things you might do to celebrate winter with the reindeer.
Draw a picture of a sleigh race. Tell a story about how you made friends with a talking reindeer on a snowy winter day!

Let's talk about snow!

Snow is frozen water or ice that forms in the air. Most snowflakes are tiny crystals with six sides. If there is a lot of water in the air and the air is very cold, the crystals may cling together. They form beautiful shapes. They fall from the sky as snow!

Dancing up a snowstorm

Do you ever look out the window in the winter and wish it would snow? Here is an activity you can try on those days when the snow just won't fall.

Have a snow dance to encourage the snow! Dress up in "snowy" outfits. Wrap yourself in white sheets, strips of tissue paper, or wear white clothes. Sing this song to tell the snow that you want it to come down.

Fall snow, fall!

Fall snow, fall gently down,
Cover the earth so bare and brown.
I want to watch the trees turn white,
I want the world to sparkle bright,
I want to make a snowman now.
Please fall snow, fall, I'll show you how!

Sing the song while you dance alone or with friends. Make up special dance movements that show the snow how it should drift, float, pelt, or flurry to the ground. Move your fingers, your arms, your head, and your legs. Sway, swing, and rock your whole body! Then run to the window. Is it snowing yet?

Make snowflakes

If you have done your best snow dance and there is still no snow, why not make your own snow? Fold a few pieces of white paper or tissue paper in half several times. Use scissors to cut the edges of the paper, leaving the folds uncut. Cut holes of different shapes into the paper. Now unfold the paper. What does your snowflake look like? Remember that snowflakes often have six sides. Can you invent new shapes for snowflakes?

Twisting and turning

Can you say this snow tongue twister quickly six times?
Shelly saw six slimy slugs snuggling in slushy snow.

An icy treat

Make edible ice. Pour any kind of juice into small plastic or paper cups. Place a clean popsicle stick in each cup and put the cups into the freezer. In several hours, take them from the freezer and carefully remove the cups from the frozen juice. Now you have icy cold popsicles for a yummy winter treat!

See them sparkle

Snowflakes falling from the sky,
Softly, slowly as a sigh.
See them sparkle, catch the light
On this winter, moonlit night.

Carnaval days with Bonhomme

Bonjour, mes amis! Welcome to Quebec City! My name is Bonhomme. I am a jolly white snowman. My red sash and hat make me impossible to miss. I am the leader of the Carnaval fun! Carnaval is the French word for carnival. Celebrate Carnaval with me.

It is cold here in Quebec City in February, but eleven days of parades, sports, and fun will keep us warm. Join me on the first Saturday evening of Carnaval, and we can watch the parades together. Carpenters have been busy building the floats. Clowns, marching bands, and characters in costumes parade with the floats through the city. Wave to the paraders and they'll wave back!

Eleven days of snow fun

Each day is full of activities. Canoes race across the ice and through the freezing water of the St. Lawrence River. If the racers slip, they are in for a cold dip! Join me in watching the National Snow Sculpture Competition. Later, we can try designing our own original snow sculpture!

Let me treat you to a breakfast of maple syrup and pancakes. After breakfast, we can cheer at the dog-sled races, the speed-skating marathon, and the acrobatic-skiing demonstration. Then we can walk up the steps to the Snow Palace. The Palace is a huge, magical structure built completely out of snow!

See you next year

Spend the eleven days of Carnaval with me. Then we'll say good-bye. But don't worry — I'll be back next year to lead you through the Carnaval festivities again!

Winter sports

Winter is a time of year when you can slip, slide, and zoom along the ice and snow. It is a time to hop on your toboggan or sled and shoot down a snow-covered hill. Watch out for the trees! You can strap on your long, thin cross-country skis and glide quietly through the fields and woods. You can put snowshoes on your feet and make huge footprints in the snow.

Zigging and zagging

Have you ever tried downhill skiing? In the winter, people compete in many downhill-skiing competitions. They zig and zag around flags on slalom courses. They ski off ramps and fly through the air for long distances. They perform acrobatics on skis!

Whizzing around

Tie up your skates and do pirouettes on the ice. Have you ever watched a speed-skating competition? The racers bend over and swing their arms. Their long skateblades glisten in the sun as they swish across the ice. Get some friends together and play hockey. Who can shoot the puck past the goalie and into the net?

Fun on the ice and snow

Join the curlers! Slide heavy round ''stones'' down the ice toward a mark in the center of a circle. Sweep the ice with a short broom so the stone will slide smoothly. Perhaps you can fish on the frozen lake on a sunny winter day. Will you catch a fish through a hole in the ice?

North American Indians used toboggans to carry supplies across the snow. Then they discovered that it was also fun to ride a toboggan down a hill! Tobogganing became a popular winter sport in Canada and the United States. Have you ever tried skijoring? Watch the Scandinavian skiers being pulled across the snow and ice by horses! Cheer the bobsled teams as they hurtle down the chutes on the mountainside. Would you like to travel that quickly?

Whichever sport you choose to try or watch, be sure to enjoy the winter air and snow!

Carnival in Trinidad

People on the Caribbean island of Trinidad have been preparing for the Carnival for months. Each year at Carnival time in February, the weather is warm. It never snows in Trinidad!

For three days of Carnival, the streets burst with color. Dancers parade to the music of steel bands. The costumes of the dancers and musicians are decorated with sequins, feathers, and crepe paper. Paraders carry flags, umbrellas, and streamers. Some wear tight, short outfits, while others wear huge, tall or wide costumes.

The people who take part in the Carnival parade have chosen a theme or idea. They have written music and songs about their theme. They have made special costumes to illustrate the theme. Now it is time for them to show off their work!

A magnificent parade

Listen to the music! A band plays songs about the travels of Marco Polo. People parade in costumes which show the many sights that Marco Polo saw on his travels. The Firecrackers of China, the Ships of Japan, and the Arabian Steeds of Persia are just some examples of the Marco Polo theme.

Another band plays songs about making waves. Dozens of people wearing sailor costumes from all over the world wiggle to these tunes. Paraders dressed as Sweet Dreams, Ghosts, Vampires, Fireflies, and Nightmares follow a band which is playing songs about the night.

Who will win?

The Carnival days of parades, music, and dancing are a time of laughter, fun, and excitement for people of all ages. Which group will win the Band-of-the-Year award? Who will have the best costume? Will it be the giant seashell or the laughing dragon? Will it be the dancing jellyfish or the disco cat? Maybe this fantastic butterfly costume will win!

Have your own Carnival!

Why don't you, your family, and your friends have a Carnival celebration in February? It's a great way to make the middle of winter a festive time. Can you think of a theme for your parade?

Dressing up

Make costumes that illustrate your Carnival theme. Wear clothes that are too big or too small. Wrap an old sheet, a blanket, or a towel around you. Decorate your costume by pinning on buttons, foil, ribbons, cutouts, doilies, or felt pieces. Make paper flowers and pin them to your costume. Make a headdress using a scarf, dishtowel, or paper towel.

The King and Queen

Now you are almost ready to begin your parade. Choose a king and queen. They can sit in a wagon decorated with crepe paper and balloons. Pull the wagon at the end of the parade line. The king and queen can wave to the crowds!

A winter Carnival song

No Carnival parade is complete without music. Have members of your parade bang pots and pans, blow whistles and recorders, and shake tambourines. Sing songs that celebrate Carnival time. Write your own songs, or write poems and recite them to your favorite background music. You might want to sing the song ''Way Down South'' while you parade!

Way Down South

1. Way down south where the bananas grow,
   A grasshopper stepped on an elephant's toe.
   The elephant cried with tears in his eyes.
   He said, ''Why don't you step on someone your own size?''

Chorus:

He said, "Walk on baby (walk on baby)"
He said, "Walk on baby (walk on baby)"
He said, "Walk on baby (walk on baby)"
He said, "Walk on baby (walk on baby)"
He said, "Walk on baby, walk on baby.
Why don't you step on someone your own size?"

Way down south where the ba- na-nas grow, A grass-hop-per stepped on an el-e-phant's toe. The el-e- phant cried with tears in his eyes. He said, "Why don't you step on someone your own size?" He said, "Walk on ba- by (walk on baby)" He said, "Walk on ba- by (walk on baby)" He said, Walk on ba- by (walk on baby)" He said, "Walk on ba- by (walk on baby)" He said, Walk on ba- by, walk on ba by. Why don't you step on someone your own size?"

2. Way up north where the people freeze,
   Your toes turn blue and you knock your knees,
   Your teeth start to chatter and you start to sneeze,
   You wish you were home in that southern breeze.

Chorus:

He said, "Walk on baby, (walk on baby)"
(repeat four more times) ...
"You wish you were home in that southern breeze."

Blah busters

Have you ever had the winter blahs? Many people are fed up with winter by the time February arrives. If you wake up one winter morning feeling this way, try these activities to cheer you up.

An invitation to play

Invite some friends over to help chase away the winter blahs. Write a funny verse in your invitation, such as this one:

Winter is here, and I must stay.
I'd rather be swimming in the bay.
But since I can't, I want to say:
Come to my house without delay,
And let's invent some games to play!

Cloud shapes

With your friends, lie face up on the floor. Close your eyes. Imagine you are looking up at a blue sky dotted with fluffy white clouds. Look at the first cloud closely. What shape do you see? Move on to the next cloud. Which animal does it resemble? Share your cloud visions with your friends. What cloud shapes did they see? How did watching the clouds make you feel?

Holiday places

Sit in a circle or in front of a fireplace with your friends. Ask them to describe a warm holiday place. How does the sun feel? How does the air smell? What sounds can they hear? What colors are the brightest? How would it feel to be there right now?

The best resort!

Invent the best holiday resort in the world. Draw the setting. Design the facilities. Will the resort have a hotel, a swimming pool, a beach area, riding stables, and hiking trails? Plan some fantastic fun-in-the-sun activities. Write an ad that would bring thousands of people to your resort.

Chasing the clouds away

If all these ideas fail to cheer you up, give in to winter! Run outside and play Chase the Clouds with your friends. Make a big circle in the snow with your footprints. Then make six lines which begin at the circle and meet at its center. All the running must take place on the spokes or the circle. The person chosen to be the Sun can tag or melt a Cloud unless the Cloud is standing in the center of the circle. Only one Cloud may be in this spot at a time, and this Cloud must leave it when another Cloud comes to take it. If the first Cloud does not give it up, he or she may be melted by the Sun.

Winter recipes

Here are some recipes that will warm your tummy! Be sure to have an adult or older friend help you use the stove or oven.

A pot of chili

What could be better than a hot bowl of chili for warming up the chilly winter?

You need:

15 mL (1 tablespoon) oil
1 medium onion, chopped
230 g (1/2 pound) ground beef (optional)
1 large can tomatoes, or 6 tomatoes, chopped
250 mL (1 cup) green pepper, chopped
1 large can kidney beans, drained
30 mL (2 tablespoons) tomato paste
10 mL (2 teaspoons) chili powder
dash of salt and pepper
pinch of paprika and garlic

Brown onions in oil. Add ground beef. Cook until brown. (If you prefer a meal without meat, leave out the beef and add more beans of your choice.) Drain fat. Add other ingredients. Cook at medium to high heat, then simmer for one hour. Stir occasionally. For hearty winter appetites, serve the chili over rice or with a stack of hot, buttered toast.

Baked Alaska

This ice-cream-and-cake dessert is both cold and hot — a perfect winter treat!

You need:

20 cm (8-inch) round cake
250 mL (8 ounces) canned raspberries
or other fruit, drained
juice from fruit
475 g (1 pound) ice cream
4 egg whites
165 mL (2/3 cup) sugar

Preheat oven to 450°F (230°C). Put cake on baking sheet. Drizzle a little fruit juice over cake. Spoon ice cream onto cake, leaving a small border around the cake uncovered. Pour fruit on top of ice cream. Place cake and ice cream in freezer.

Now make meringue. Beat egg whites until stiff. Beat in sugar, one spoonful at a time, until egg whites stand in stiff peaks. Remove cake from freezer and cover with meringue. Be sure the meringue completely covers the cake, ice cream, and fruit, sealing the sides completely. Place in oven. Remove when meringue begins to brown. Serve Baked Alaska immediately.

The biggest snowman ever

This morning, this morning, I ran outside.
The sun was shining, shining bright.
Snow and more snow was here, was there,
What a winterful, wonderful sight!

I said to myself, ''Yes, this is the day,
The day that the world will see
The biggest snowman that ever was made,
Much bigger than ever could be!''

I ran outside, I looked at the snow.
Then I took a deep breath and began.
I rolled and rolled and rolled that snow
Until I made the biggest snowman,

The biggest snowman that ever was,
The biggest there'll ever be.
He was bigger than Mom, he was bigger than Dad,
He was a hundred times bigger than me.

I crawled on up and stood on his head,
I looked all around, near and far.
I could see all the mountains, I could see all the seas,
I looked up — I could see every star!

The moon was so big and so bright and so near,
I could reach out and poke it, I bet.
And the sun was so close, it was making me hot,
In fact, it was making me sweat!

I started to drip, and I started to drop,
I took off my coat and my hat.
Then I suddenly noticed
    the snowman sweat too,
And that, let me tell you, was that!

For sooner than now and a little after then
The biggest snowman there'll ever be
Began quickly to melt, to shrink,
    to dissolve,
And on top of that snowman was me!

"Good-bye to the mountains,
    to the seas, to the moon,
Good-bye to the stars, to the sun.
Good-bye to the biggest snowman,
There'll never be a bigger one!"

53

Good-bye to winter

Here comes the spring. The snow is still falling, but the sun shines longer each day. The wind is still howling, but the sap is beginning to flow in the trees. Nature is coming to life again.

In Switzerland, young people say good-bye to winter and welcome spring by dressing up as cowherds. Some wear bells across their chests. Others are the cows! They clang the cowbells they wear around their necks. They follow the herdsmen from home to home. Everyone sings:

The first of March, the first of April,
Let the cows out of the stable.
Grow grass, grow!
Go away snow, go!

Hello to spring

In the far north, the sun has not been seen all winter. Then it peeks over the horizon for the first time. When this happens, the Inuit celebrate the return of the sun and the ending of winter. The children run from home to home putting out all the lamps. They light the lamps with flames taken from new fires to show that spring is a time of new light!

Come soon please!

Old Man Winter is leaving now,
And spring is on its way.
We just can't wait to wake up to
That first warm, sunny day.
We've loved the ice, we've loved the cold,
We've even loved the snow,
But now it's time to wave good-bye
As Old Man Winter goes.
Welcome the rainbows, flowers, and grass,
Welcome the buds on the trees,
Welcome the puddles, butterflies, and clouds,
Welcome spring! And come soon please!

Index

1112131415 LB Printed in the U.S.A. 9876543